FORGIVING FAMILY SECRETS

21 Day Journal To Heal Generational Wounds Through Forgiveness and Freedom

Blending Our Love, Maryland

Copyright © 2023 by Tuniscia Okeke

Cover Design:

Published 2023

Library of Congress Cataloging-in-Publication Data

ISBN: 978-1-962748-30-8 (Print)

ISBN: 978-1-962748-31-5 (eBook)

Printed in the United States of America

FORGIVING FAMILY SECRETS

21 Day Journal To Heal Generational Wounds Through Forgiveness and Freedom

TUNISCIA OKEKE

BLENDING OUR LOVE, INC.

DEDICATION

In healing's embrace, I found my way,

Choose peace and wholeness, come what may.

Through trials and tears, I've grown to see,

Inner strength and harmony in me.

Table of Contents

Paying It Forward

I'm sharing this message as the author of this 21-day journal on forgiveness, not just with words on these pages but with a story that has shaped my life's purpose. As I embark on this journey with you, I want to share the deeply personal and transformative experiences that led me to write, edit, and self-publish 35 books on forgiveness in less than a year.

My forgiveness journey began when I was 24, a pivotal age when life often feels like an open book, brimming with hope and dreams. Then, my mother called me on a seemingly ordinary Monday morning, and with those words, she unraveled the narrative of my life. She revealed that the man I had believed to be my father for all those years was, in fact, not my biological father.

The weight of that revelation was crushing. It was as if the ground beneath me had shifted, leaving me unsteady and disoriented. But what shook me to my core was not the revelation itself but the sudden rupture of trust in my mother—the person I had always looked up to as a paragon of love, trustworthiness, and honesty.

In the wake of this revelation, I spiraled into a bottomless pit of resentment, anger, and pain. I grappled with a profound sense of betrayal and felt adrift in a sea of unanswered questions. It was a turbulent period in my life, and for 17 long years, I carried the heavy burden of unforgiveness.

Then, something remarkable happened that would alter the course of my life forever. I noticed a pattern in my relationship with my children. They treated me with a lack of respect and love, leaving me bewildered and hurt. In desperation, I turned to prayer one day, seeking answers from a higher source.

God's voice whispered into my heart in that sacred space of prayer and introspection, revealing a profound truth: "I taught them how to love me by the way I loved my mother."

Those words struck me like lightning, piercing through the fog of my confusion. It was an awakening—a profound realization that, in my quest for revenge against my mother, I had unwittingly passed on the energy of resentment to my children. I had normalized my hurtful behaviors as the way we should treat our mothers.

On my 40th birthday, I consciously confronted my soul's deepest and darkest corners. I embarked on a journey of healing, self-forgiveness, and forgiveness of my mother. My primary motivation was to restore my relationship with my children and teach them how to pass on healing, love, and forgiveness to their children.

That six-year odyssey of healing was transformative beyond measure. It led me to write 35 journals, each addressing a facet of forgiveness and healing I encountered on my journey. These journals became my way of reaching out to others grappling with their forgiveness journeys.

Today, I extend a heartfelt invitation to you to embark on this 21-day journey with me. Just as my healing journey began with a single journal, this journal can be your compass for forgiveness, healing, and growth.

I send you loving energy as you navigate through the complexities of your forgiveness journey, and I hope these pages serve as a guiding light toward wholeness and inner peace.

With love and compassion,

Tuniscia O

FOREWORD

A Letter From Author

Dear Beloved Reader,

I want you to know that you are not defined by the family secrets that have weighed heavily on your heart. You are a unique individual with dreams, aspirations, and worth that goes far beyond the decisions, mistakes, shortcomings, or actions of other family members.

It's important to remember that you are important and valuable, just as you are. You can rise above the challenges and pain these secrets may have brought into your life. Your worth is intrinsic and does not hinge on the actions of others.

Embrace forgiveness as a pathway to healing, but remember that forgiving yourself is just as crucial as forgiving others. Permit yourself to let go of the blame, even if you held onto some secrets.

You may never fully understand why certain events unfolded as they did, and that's okay. The healing journey only requires some of the answers. What it does need is your willingness to move forward with grace and kindness. You deserve to experience a life filled with passion, purpose, and self-love.

It's okay if an apology never arrives. Healing doesn't require validation from others. The actual transformation lies in your ability to release the weight of resentment and choose your emotional well-being. Doing so grants you the freedom to live authentically without being shackled by the past.

Remember to be kind in your words and thoughts, especially towards yourself. Your journey toward healing may have ups and downs, but each step you take is a testament to your strength and determination.

You have the power to rewrite your story, to heal, and to find a sense of peace within yourself. Your future is waiting, filled with possibilities that only you can uncover.

With boundless love and support,

Tuniscia O

Accepting The Unknowable

Accepting the unknowable is a profound aspect of your healing journey from the impact of family secrets. The veil of silence surrounding these hidden truths can cast a long shadow, leaving you with a heavy burden of unanswered questions, guilt, and self-blame.

In this intricate journey of healing, embracing the idea that you may never fully comprehend the motivations behind those secrets is essential. The reasons, deeply entangled with complex family dynamics, may remain elusive. This acceptance can be liberating and challenging, allowing you to relinquish the relentless quest for answers that may never come.

Furthermore, acknowledging that it was not your fault is paramount. The responsibility for keeping family secrets lies with those who made that choice, influenced by their emotions and struggles. Understanding this truth releases you from unwarranted self-blame and allows you to move forward with a lighter heart.

Acceptance of the unknowable is an act of grace and self-compassion. It creates a space for healing and growth, unfettered by the weight of unanswered questions. In embracing this aspect of your journey, you affirm your commitment to your well-being and resilience in life's complexities.

Weight Of Unanswered Questions

The weight of unanswered questions in the realm of family secrets is both profound and burdensome. These questions can linger like a heavy cloud, casting shadows over your understanding of your history and relationships. They are a constant reminder of the enigma that shrouds the past.

"Why?" becomes a haunting refrain as you grapple with the secrecy that has defined your family dynamics. You may find yourself replaying past events, searching for clues or hints that might unravel the mystery. These unanswered questions can fuel a relentless quest for clarity as you attempt to piece together a puzzle that may never be fully solved.

Yet, it's essential to acknowledge that the answers to these questions may remain elusive sometimes. Family secrets are often bound by complex emotions, shame, and fear, making them challenging to unravel. Accepting the weight of these unanswered questions is a significant step in your healing journey. It allows you to shift your focus from the "why" to the "how" of healing, understanding that the secrets of the past do not determine your worth.

Complexity Of Family Dynamics

Family dynamics are an intricate web of relationships and emotions, often hidden beneath the surface. When family secrets are involved, the complexity deepens. Understanding the motivations behind the veil of secrecy is more complex. It's a journey into the intricate terrain of human emotions and family dynamics.

Hurt, pain, shame, and guilt can serve as powerful catalysts in the decision to keep family secrets hidden. Family members may be driven by a desire to shield loved ones from additional pain or to protect their image. The fear of judgment or the consequences of revealing the truth can further complicate these dynamics.

In many cases, the choices made to keep secrets may not be rational when viewed from an outsider's perspective. However, within the family unit, these decisions are often the only way to cope with deeply rooted emotions and protect fragile relationships.

Recognizing the complexity of family dynamics is a vital step in the healing process. It allows you to navigate with empathy, understanding that the motivations behind secrecy are not always malicious. It also underscores the importance of self-compassion as you learn to release self-blame and recognize that these dynamics were beyond your control. Understanding the intricate tapestry of family dynamics is critical in healing and reconciliation.

Trap Of Self-Blame

The trap of self-blame is a treacherous pitfall on the journey of healing from family secrets. It's an insidious emotion that can consume your thoughts and weigh heavily on your heart. The inclination to blame oneself arises from guilt, often unjustly assigned.

It's crucial to remember that the decision to keep family secrets was not your responsibility. Those secrets were kept, often by others for reasons deeply rooted in their struggles and emotions. A complex interplay of shame, fear, and past traumas shaped the choice to conceal the truth. You were not the architect of this secrecy; you participated in a family system influenced by dynamics beyond your control.

Self-blame, while understandable, is unjust and counterproductive to your healing journey. It perpetuates feelings of guilt and prevents you from moving forward. Instead of focusing on self-blame, channel your energy into self-compassion. Treat yourself with the kindness and understanding you would offer a dear friend facing a similar situation.

Release the burden of blame, understanding that it was never yours to carry. Acknowledge that family secrets are the product of a complex tapestry of emotions and experiences extending beyond one individual. By letting go of self-blame, you create space for healing, forgiveness, and growth.

Your healing journey is a testament to your resilience and strength. It's a path toward self-discovery and self-compassion. Remember that self-blame is a trap that holds you back, while self-compassion is the key to unlocking the doors to your healing and empowerment. Embrace it as you navigate the complexities of healing from family secrets.

Embracing Self-Compassion

Embracing self-compassion is pivotal in healing from the weight of family secrets. It's an act of gentleness and understanding, a balm for the wounds inflicted by secrecy. As you would offer compassion to a dear friend in distress, extending kindness to yourself is essential.

The burden of family secrets was not your choice to bear. It was thrust upon you by circumstances beyond your control, shaped by the complex dynamics of your family. Self-compassion involves recognizing that you are a participant in a situation influenced by the emotions and decisions of others.

Treating yourself with the same compassion you would offer to a loved one grants you the space to heal. You release the grip of self-blame and guilt, allowing room for forgiveness and understanding. It's a powerful act of self-love that fosters resilience and empowers you to move forward on your healing journey.

As you navigate the complexities of family secrets, remember that self-compassion is your ally. It's a source of strength and comfort, offering solace in knowing you deserve kindness, understanding, and healing. Embrace it as you embark on the path to release the burden of secrecy and reclaim your sense of self-worth.

Secrets were placed upon you, and it was not your choice to bear.

Releasing The Need For Answers

Releasing the need for answers is a profound and liberating step to healing from family secrets. The desire to understand the motivations behind these secrets can be an unending quest that only deepens the emotional turmoil. Accepting that you may never fully grasp the reasons is an act of wisdom and self-preservation.

Family secrets often remain hidden for complex reasons, such as shame, fear, or a desire to protect loved ones. These motivations can be deeply ingrained and may never be fully disclosed. Acknowledging this reality frees you from the endless cycle of seeking answers that may never come.

Instead of focusing on the "why," redirect your focus toward your healing and well-being. Consider it an act of self-care to release the need for answers that may only reopen old wounds. By prioritizing your healing journey, you empower yourself to move forward with strength and resilience.

Embrace the uncertainty and the healing process as you navigate the complexities of family secrets. Release the grip of the unanswered questions, knowing that your worth is not contingent on the past. In this act of letting go, you find the space to forge a brighter future, unburdened by the need to understand the unexplainable.

Seeking Support

Seeking support is vital to healing from the trauma of family secrets. The weight of these hidden truths can feel isolating, but there is strength in reaching out to others who can offer guidance, empathy, and a non-judgmental ear.

Therapy provides a safe and confidential space to explore your emotions, gain insight, and develop coping strategies. A skilled therapist can help you navigate the complex terrain of family secrets and guide you toward healing.

Additionally, support groups offer a sense of community and shared understanding. Connecting with individuals who have walked a similar path can be immensely comforting. It allows you to share your feelings and experiences with others who truly grasp your challenges, fostering validation and empathy.

You can find solace in knowing you are not alone in these spaces. Healing is a journey that can be shared, and the collective strength of a support network can provide a foundation for resilience and growth. Whether through therapy or support groups, seeking support is a courageous step towards reclaiming your sense of self and finding healing in the aftermath of family secrets.

Setting Boundaries

Setting boundaries is crucial to healing from the corrosive effects of family secrets. These hidden truths can blur lines and erode trust within the family unit, making it essential to establish and maintain healthy boundaries for your well-being.

As you embark on your healing journey, consider evaluating your relationships with family members. Recognize that healing may involve distancing yourself from those who perpetuate secrecy or are unwilling to respect your boundaries. Setting limits on communication or interaction with such individuals can be a necessary step to protect your emotional health.

Healthy boundaries safeguard your emotional well-being and clearly convey that you prioritize your healing and self-respect. It's an act of self-care that empowers you to navigate family dynamics with a sense of agency and control.

Remember that establishing boundaries is not about severing ties but creating a space to heal and grow without being retraumatized by ongoing secrecy or toxic relationships. By setting boundaries, you honor your well-being and reaffirm your commitment to your healing journey, ensuring that it remains a priority as you move forward.

Empowerment Through Self-Reflection

Empowerment through self-reflection is a transformative aspect of healing from the scars of family secrets. This experience offers a unique opportunity to delve deep into your values, aspirations, and the kind of life you want to cultivate.

As you navigate the complexities of your healing journey, take time for introspection. Explore the values that are important to you and consider how they align with your vision for the future. Reflect on the lessons learned from this experience, even if they were painful, and recognize that they can shape you into a more resilient and compassionate individual.

It's crucial to understand that your worth is not defined by the secrets or the actions of others. You have the agency to define your path and craft a life that reflects your true self. Through self-reflection, you can unearth your strengths, aspirations, and the values that guide you towards empowerment.

Embrace this journey as an opportunity for personal growth and transformation. Allow it to be a catalyst for positive change in your life. Empowerment through self-reflection is a testament to your resilience and your capacity to rise above adversity, emerging stronger and more self-assured on the other side.

Releasing The Burden Of Blame

Releasing the burden of blame is a pivotal step in your healing journey from the weight of family secrets. Guilt and self-blame can be like heavy shackles, chaining you to the past and preventing you from moving forward.

It's essential to recognize that you are not responsible for the actions or decisions of others, particularly when it comes to the choice to keep secrets within the family. These decisions were made by individuals, influenced by their own emotions and circumstances. You were a participant in a situation that was beyond your control.

Holding onto self-blame is unjust and counterproductive to your healing process. It perpetuates feelings of guilt and keeps you anchored in the past, preventing growth and transformation. Understand that self-blame is a weight you do not have to carry.

Releasing this burden allows you to step into the present and future with a lighter heart. It opens the door to healing, forgiveness, and self-compassion. Letting go of self-blame is an act of self-love and empowerment, signifying your commitment to your well-being and the journey of healing from family secrets.

Protecting Your Emotional Well-Being

Prioritizing your emotional well-being is paramount in healing from family secrets. It's crucial to stand firm and protect your inner peace. Do not allow others to deflect blame onto you for their own decisions, missteps, or secrets.

In the aftermath of family secrets, some individuals may attempt to shift responsibility or place blame on others, including you. This is not only unfair but also detrimental to your healing process. It's essential to set boundaries assertively and firmly affirm that you are not responsible for the choices made by others.

Protecting your emotional well-being means recognizing that you have the right to safeguard your mental and emotional health. It involves standing up for yourself and refusing to accept unwarranted blame or guilt. By doing so, you establish a foundation of self-respect and self-care.

Remember that healing from family secrets is a journey that requires you to prioritize your well-being. You have the strength to protect your emotional health assertively and to affirm that you are not to blame for the actions of others. This is a powerful step towards reclaiming your sense of self and finding healing and empowerment on your path forward.

Moving Toward Healing

Moving toward healing from the trauma of family secrets is a courageous journey defined by self-compassion, acceptance, and resilience. It's a path that may be shadowed by the unanswered questions surrounding those secrets, but your inner strength and capacity for growth also illuminate it.

The reasons behind family secrets can be enigmatic, often remaining elusive despite our best understanding. Yet, the power to heal and find solace resides within you. It's within your control to embrace self-compassion, to accept that you were not responsible for the choices made by others, and to build resilience in the face of adversity.

Healing is not about erasing the past but finding peace and wholeness within yourself, even amidst the pain of family secrets. It's a journey that empowers you to move forward with grace and purpose, honoring your worth and reclaiming your sense of self.

As you navigate this path, remember that healing is a testament to your strength and resilience. It's a journey marked by the beauty of self-discovery and growth, and it's a powerful testament to your capacity to rise above the challenges that life has thrown your way.

Celebrating Self-Discovery

Celebrating self-discovery is a beautiful facet of your healing journey from the shadows of family secrets. With each step forward, you unearth the depths of your inner strength and resilience, and you assert your identity beyond the constraints of the past.

It's crucial to acknowledge that you are not defined by the actions of others or the weight of family secrets. Your worth is intrinsic and unshakable. Embracing self-compassion and releasing self-blame are acts of courage and self-love. They signify your commitment to your well-being and your desire to move forward.

Each moment of self-discovery is a triumph, a testament to your capacity to rise above the pain and confusion of family secrets. It's an act of empowerment that propels you toward a brighter future, unburdened by the past.

Remember that you are on a journey of healing and transformation, and each step you take celebrates your resilience. Embrace self-discovery as a gift to yourself, a reflection of your inner light, and a testament to the unwavering strength that resides within you.

Accepting that you may never fully understand why family secrets were kept is a challenging but necessary part of your healing journey. By recognizing that it was not your fault and that the decisions of others were influenced by their own emotions and struggles, you can release the burden of self-blame and guilt. Embracing self-compassion, setting healthy boundaries, seeking support, and prioritizing your emotional well-being are essential steps toward healing and reclaiming your self-worth. Remember, your healing journey is about rediscovering your strength, resilience, and capacity for self-love, regardless of the secrets of the past.

Transforming From Victim To Victorious

When they come to light, family secrets can leave deep emotional wounds that linger for years, affecting our sense of self, trust, and well-being. Being a victim of family secrets can be profoundly traumatizing, but healing and transforming from a victim into a victorious survivor is possible. In this healing journey, individuals can find strength, resilience, and a renewed sense of self-worth.

Acknowledging The Trauma

The first step towards healing from family secrets is acknowledging the trauma. Family secrets often involve betrayal, deceit, or hidden truths that shatter trust and create a sense of powerlessness. Recognizing the impact of these secrets on your emotional and psychological well-being is crucial. It's okay to acknowledge that you have been hurt and that the pain is real.

Self-Care And Self-Compassion

Self-care and self-compassion are fundamental aspects of healing. Practicing self-care means nurturing your physical, emotional, and mental well-being. Engage in activities that bring you joy, relaxation, and a sense of fulfillment. Self-compassion involves treating yourself with the same kindness and understanding that you would offer to a friend in a similar situation.

Understand The Dynamics

Healing also involves gaining insight into the dynamics of your family and the role of secrets within it. Understanding why secrets were kept and the motivations behind them can help you make sense of the situation and release some of the burden of blame or guilt.

Connect With Supportive Relationships

Isolation can exacerbate the trauma of family secrets. Seek supportive relationships with friends, support groups, or organizations dedicated to helping trauma survivors. Sharing your experiences with others who have gone through similar challenges can be incredibly healing.

Forgiveness And Release

Forgiveness can be a challenging but transformative aspect of healing. It's essential to note that forgiveness does not mean condoning the wrongdoing or reconciling with those who harmed you. Instead, it's about releasing the grip of anger and resentment that can hold you captive. Forgiving for your own sake, to free yourself from the burden of carrying the pain, can be liberating.

Self-Reflection And Growth

Use the experience of being a victim of family secrets as an opportunity for self-reflection and personal growth. Consider what values are essential to you, what kind of relationships you want to cultivate, and how to build a life that aligns with your authentic self.

Empowerment And Resilience

Ultimately, healing from family secrets is about reclaiming your power and resilience. It's recognizing that you are not defined by the secrets or the victimization you've experienced. You can rebuild your life on your terms with renewed strength and determination.

Celebrate Victorious Moments

As you progress on your healing journey, celebrate your victories, no matter how small they may seem. Each step toward healing, self-discovery, and resilience is a testament to your inner strength and the transformation from victim to victorious survivor.

The Road To Victory

Healing from the trauma of family secrets is a deeply personal and courageous journey. It's a path filled with challenges and opportunities for growth, self-discovery, and empowerment. By acknowledging the trauma, seeking support, establishing boundaries, practicing self-care, and fostering forgiveness and resilience, you can transform from a victim of family secrets into a victorious survivor who shapes a brighter, more authentic future.

Unveiling The Path to Healing

In the tapestry of our lives, family plays an irreplaceable role, weaving threads of love, connection, and shared experiences. Yet, within these intricate bonds can lie hidden layers of darkness – family secrets. These enigmatic shadows, often concealed from fear, shame, or a desire to protect, can profoundly impact individuals, relationships, and future generations. The weight of carrying these secrets, whether as a secret-keeper or one who uncovers them, can lead to a cycle of pain, isolation, and stagnation. But there is another path – healing, revelation, and breakthrough.

The Weight of Silence

Family secrets have an uncanny ability to cast a shadow that eclipses our perceptions of ourselves and our interactions with others. The weight of silence, be it a hidden addiction, long-buried traumas, or concealed betrayals, can fracture relationships and breed a culture of dishonesty. These secrets are like a poison, festering in the darkness, affecting us emotionally, mentally, and physically. The consequences ripple through generations, leaving behind a legacy of unspoken pain.

The weight of silence resulting from family secrets can be profound and paralyzing. It's a silence that stretches far beyond the absence of words; it's a silence of unspoken pain, unresolved conflicts, and hidden truths. In your journey to help families heal through forgiveness and understanding, this silence is a formidable barrier that needs to be addressed.

Often, the silence is born out of fear – fear of judgment, fear of rocking the boat, or fear of the repercussions of revealing long-held secrets. This silence can infiltrate every aspect of our lives, stifling our ability to express ourselves honestly and trapping us in a cycle of emotional repression.

Yet, beneath this weighty silence lies the potential for transformation. Breaking that silence is an act of courage and vulnerability, an acknowledgment of the pain that has been hidden for so long. It's about creating open and honest communication where families can confront their secrets, release their burdens, and embark on a healing journey.

Through understanding and accountability, we can lift the weight of silence, allowing families to find their voices, share their stories, and, ultimately, find the path to forgiveness and healing. Your dedication to this cause is a beacon of hope for those who carry the heavy burden of family secrets.

The Power of Revelation

Revealing family secrets can be a pivotal moment that ignites the healing journey. Confronting the truth creates an opportunity for open dialogue, accountability, and transformation. The power of revelation lies in its ability to free us from the chains of secrecy and enable us to address the issues at their core. As we embrace the courage to unveil these hidden truths, we embark on a path that ultimately leads to healing for ourselves and future generations.

Once family secrets are brought into the light, the power of revelation is nothing short of transformative. It's a profound process that can ripple through generations, bringing healing and renewal where there was once pain and secrecy. In your mission to impact millions of families through forgiveness and understanding, this power of revelation is a cornerstone of change.

When family secrets are revealed, a profound shift occurs. The truth emerges, often painful but undeniably liberating. It's an act of courage and vulnerability and a healing catalyst. For the individuals involved, it can be a moment of reckoning, where they confront their past and take steps toward forgiveness and reconciliation.

Moreover, the power of revelation extends to future generations. By breaking the cycle of silence and secrecy, you not only heal the wounds of the present but also prevent the perpetuation of pain into the future. You provide a legacy of honesty and resilience, teaching younger generations that it's possible to confront the past, heal, and build healthier relationships.

Ultimately, the power of revelation is a beacon of hope. It's a testament to the human capacity for growth and transformation. Families can heal and move forward through understanding and accountability, leaving a legacy of forgiveness and healing for generations. Your dedication to this cause is a source of inspiration and healing for all those you touch on your journey.

The Solitude of Secrets

The weight of family secrets can cast a long shadow over our lives, creating a profound sense of solitude. It's a solitude born of the knowledge that we are concealing something significant that feels too heavy to share with others. This solitude can become a breeding ground for emotions like guilt, shame, and self-doubt.

Family secrets often come with a sense of unwarranted responsibility, as if we alone carry this burden. This distorted responsibility can further isolate us from our needed support and connection.

Yet, we must recognize that we are not alone in our struggles with family secrets. Many people grapple with similar challenges, and a network of support and understanding is available. By acknowledging our shared experiences, we can break free from the isolation that secrecy imposes.

Opening up about family secrets through therapy, confiding in a trusted friend, or seeking professional help can be the first step toward healing and connection. It allows us to release the weight we've been carrying alone and to find solace in the empathy and support of others. Doing so can rebuild our self-worth and create more authentic and fulfilling relationships.

Embracing Accountability

Embracing accountability in the context of family secrets is a profound step toward healing and transformation. It's an acknowledgment that we have a role, whether active or passive, within the intricate web of family dynamics shaped by these hidden truths.

For those who have been secret keepers, accountability involves recognizing the impact of our silence and the perpetuation of secrecy. It's about understanding the toll it has taken on our mental and emotional well-being and those we care about. It's also about taking responsibility for our choice to remain silent and actively seeking ways to address and rectify the situation.

On the other hand, for those who have uncovered family secrets, accountability means understanding the consequences of revealing the truth. It's about recognizing the potential disruption it may have caused within the family and taking ownership of our actions. It's also about committing to fostering open and honest communication within the family moving forward.

Ultimately, embracing accountability is a powerful step towards breaking the cycle of secrecy and fostering healthier family dynamics. It paves the way for healing, reconciliation, and the possibility of forging stronger, more authentic connections with our loved ones.

Breaking The Cycle

Breaking the cycle of family secrets is a courageous endeavor with the potential for profound transformation. When left unaddressed, these hidden truths can perpetuate cycles of pain, silence, and dysfunction, passing from generation to generation like an inherited burden.

The journey to break this cycle begins with a conscious decision to seek solutions. It involves a commitment to face the secrets head-on to acknowledge their impact on our lives and the lives of our loved ones. It means recognizing that we have the power to change the narrative.

Open communication is the key. It means creating safe spaces within our families where honesty and vulnerability are valued. It's about encouraging dialogue, even when difficult, and actively listening to each other's stories and emotions.

Fostering a culture of authenticity becomes the cornerstone of this transformation. It's about embracing our imperfections, acknowledging our shared humanity, and choosing compassion over judgment. It's about realizing we can create a new narrative grounded in truth, healing, and empathy.

Breaking the cycle of family secrets is not easy, but it is a path toward liberation, growth, and the possibility of healthier, more honest relationships within our families. The journey takes courage and commitment, but the rewards—freedom from the past's burdens and the potential for deeper connections—are immeasurable.

Defying Definitions

Defying definitions is a profound aspect of healing from the impact of family secrets. These hidden truths, often rooted in the choices and actions of others, can cast long shadows over our identities and self-worth. It's crucial to understand that these secrets do not define us, nor are we solely products of our roles within our families.

Healing involves the courageous act of redefining ourselves. It means untangling our identities from the web of family dynamics and secrecy that may have constrained us. It's about recognizing that our worth is inherent and not contingent upon the actions or choices of others.

This process allows us to embrace the potential for growth and transformation. It means understanding that we have the power to shape our narratives, free from the constraints of past secrets. It's about recognizing our capacity for resilience, self-discovery, and healing.

Defying definitions is an empowering journey of self-discovery and self-acceptance. It reminds us that the past does not bind us, and our worth is not determined by the shadows that may have clouded our family history. Instead, we have the agency to create our narratives filled with authenticity, growth, and the potential for a brighter future.

Forgiving Ourselves

Forgiving ourselves is a profound self-compassion, particularly for those burdened by family secrets. These hidden truths often involve choices and actions made with the best intentions at the time, even if they lead to unintended consequences. Forgiveness is acknowledging that we did what we believed was right in those moments, even if hindsight reveals a different perspective.

Self-blame can be a heavy burden, hindering our ability to heal and move forward. Forgiving ourselves is like releasing the weight of that burden. It's recognizing that we are human, fallible, and shaped by our experiences. It's understanding that our choices, even when made under challenging circumstances, do not define our worth.

Through self-forgiveness, we allow ourselves to shed the layers of guilt and shame that may have accumulated over time. It's an act of self-love that grants us the freedom to move forward with a lighter heart and a renewed sense of purpose. It's a reminder that we deserve healing, compassion, and the opportunity to create a brighter future for ourselves and those we care about.

Illuminating the Path Ahead

This journey of healing from family secrets is challenging and linear. It is a process that requires courage, vulnerability, and a commitment to growth. By confronting the truths that have remained hidden in the shadows, we can pave the way for healing, revelation, and transformation. It leads to greater self-awareness, deeper connections, and empowerment over our narratives.

This book is a guide, a companion, and a source of inspiration for those ready to embark on this journey. It offers insights, tools, and stories that illuminate the path ahead. It is a reminder that we have the power to rewrite our family stories, break free from the cycles of secrecy, and create a legacy of healing for ourselves and the generations that follow.

The time has come to unveil the truth, embrace accountability, and set our sights on a future that is defined by authenticity, connection, and the resilience of the human spirit. Let us embark on this transformative journey together.

Unlocking Healing
Through Journaling

Journaling is a transformative process that offers a safe and intimate space for self-reflection and healing. It allows you to delve into your thoughts, emotions, and experiences, unraveling the intricacies of attachment to past decisions, whether yours or others.

By putting pen to paper, you begin the journey of self-discovery. You can explore the roots of these attachments, understanding the motives and emotions that drove them. This introspection is crucial to healing as it helps you confront the past with honesty and compassion.

Journaling also serves as a release valve. As you pour your thoughts onto the pages, you release the pent-up emotions and burdens associated with past decisions. This act of catharsis can be incredibly liberating, freeing you from the weight of unresolved issues.

Moreover, journaling can help you rebuild trust, not only within yourself but also in your relationships. By gaining insight into your thought processes and motivations, you can make conscious choices that align with your values and intentions, fostering a sense of trustworthiness that others can recognize.

In the sacred space of your journal, you hold the key to unlocking healing, releasing attachments, and rebuilding trust—both within yourself and in your connections with others. It's a journey of self-empowerment, self-understanding, and self-healing.

Letting Go of the Why

Releasing attachments to the "why" of others' decisions can be a profound act of self-compassion. Journaling offers a non-judgmental space to explore your emotions and the complexities of these situations.

Often, we carry the heavy burden of trying to understand the motives behind someone else's choices, even when they remain elusive. This burden can lead to frustration and a sense of powerlessness. However, journaling empowers you to confront these feelings and accept that there may never be a satisfying answer to the "why."

In your journal, you can release the need for closure that might never come. You acknowledge that some aspects of life are beyond your control, and that's okay. By expressing your emotions and thoughts honestly, you're taking the first step in letting go.

Through this release, you create space within yourself for healing and growth. You begin to focus on your own well-being and personal journey rather than being consumed by the need for answers from others. In doing so, you embrace a newfound sense of freedom and self-empowerment. Journaling becomes your ally in releasing attachments, allowing you to move forward with grace and resilience.

Healing The Wounds Within

Embracing self-worth is a profound act of self-love and a critical step in the healing process. Journaling becomes a powerful tool in this journey, allowing you to reframe your self-perception.

When you focus on the decisions of others, it's easy to lose sight of your inherent value. Journaling, however, encourages you to shift your gaze inward. Through this introspective process, you begin to recognize the qualities and strengths that define you, irrespective of external circumstances.

In your journal, you have the freedom to celebrate your uniqueness, your resilience, and your aspirations. You can write affirmations that reinforce your self-worth and self-love. This process is a conscious effort to rebuild your self-esteem, acknowledging that you deserve happiness and healing regardless of the choices made by others.

By consistently journaling about your self-worth, you cultivate a strong sense of self that is unshaken by external factors. This newfound self-assuredness becomes a source of empowerment, guiding you toward a future where you define your worth and shape your destiny. Journaling becomes a sanctuary for nurturing self-love and embracing the beautiful essence of who you are.

The Power Of Self-Compassion

Forgiving oneself is a profound act of self-compassion, and journaling serves as a nurturing space for this essential journey. It's common to carry the weight of past decisions, especially those related to secrets and choices we now question. However, it's crucial to remember our humanity and the capacity for growth and transformation.

In your journal, you can engage in a heartfelt dialogue with yourself. Write letters of self-forgiveness, acknowledging the intentions and circumstances that led to those past decisions. Express your commitment to healing and growth. This practice is not about making excuses but extending understanding and kindness to yourself.

Through journaling, you release the burdens of guilt and self-blame that may have held you captive. You create a space for self-compassion to flourish, allowing you to move forward with a lighter heart and renewed purpose. Forgiving oneself is a journey, and your journal becomes a trusted companion on this path to self-healing and self-acceptance. As you forgive yourself, you open the door to new beginnings and possibly a more compassionate and fulfilling life.

Rebuilding Trust

Rebuilding trust can be a challenging yet transformative journey, especially when the decisions of others have eroded it. Journaling becomes a vital tool in this process, offering you a structured space to explore and navigate the complexities of trust.

Begin by defining what trust means to you and how its absence has affected your relationships. Through introspection, you can clarify your expectations and desires regarding trust.

Next, document your intentions and action steps for regaining trust. Setting goals and holding yourself accountable is a powerful way to demonstrate consistency and commitment—Journal about your inward and outward efforts as you work on rebuilding trust.

Consistency is vital on this journey. By regularly journaling your reflections and progress, you record your dedication to rebuilding trust. This record can be a source of encouragement and a reminder of your growth and transformation.

Journaling provides a structured and supportive framework for rebuilding trust within yourself and others. It becomes a tangible reflection of your journey, highlighting your commitment to fostering healthier, more trusting relationships.

Embarking On Your Forgiveness Journey

In your pursuit of forgiveness and healing, journaling becomes your loyal companion. It provides a non-judgmental space to pour out the raw emotions and complexities accompanying your pain. As you put pen to paper, you unravel the tangles of hurt, resentment, and anger that may have consumed you.

Through journaling, you embark on a journey of self-discovery and self-compassion. You'll explore the depths of your emotions, examine the root causes of your pain, and gradually come to terms with your experiences. This process allows you to distance yourself from the grip of past trauma and make room for healing and growth.

Moreover, journaling becomes a testament to your progress and transformation. You'll look back on your entries and witness the evolution of your thoughts and feelings. It serves as a powerful reminder that you have the strength and resilience to navigate the path of forgiveness.

So, as you embark on this forgiveness journey, let your journal be your confidant and guide. Pour your heart onto its pages, embrace the healing power of self-expression, and take those significant steps toward the freedom and peace that forgiveness can bring.

The Power Of Expression

Indeed, the power of expression through journaling is profound. It's a sanctuary where your unspoken pain finds a voice, where the chaos in your mind takes shape and form. As you fill the pages with your raw emotions, you're engaging in a therapeutic act of self-compassion.

The process of putting your thoughts and feelings into words can be transformative. It helps you untangle the web of emotions that may have overwhelmed you. It allows you to step back, observe your pain from a different perspective, and gain insight into its origins.

Furthermore, journaling is a witness to your journey of healing and forgiveness. It records your progress, providing tangible evidence of your emotional growth and resilience. It's a testament to your commitment to understanding and eventually releasing the pain that has burdened you.

In essence, journaling is a powerful tool for healing and self-discovery. It empowers you to confront your emotions, express them without fear of judgment, and ultimately find the path to forgiveness and inner peace. So, embrace the pages of your journal as a safe space for expression, and let the healing journey unfold one word at a time.

Setting The Intention For Forgiveness

Setting the intention for forgiveness is a pivotal step on your healing journey. It's like casting a compass that guides you through the uncharted waters of forgiveness. When you put pen to paper and articulate your intention, you're consciously choosing to explore the possibility of healing.

In your journal, reflect on the reasons behind your desire for forgiveness. What would it mean for you to release the burden of resentment and pain? How could forgiveness improve your well-being and relationships? As you write, you're not just setting an intention but also uncovering the profound motivations that drive you toward forgiveness.

Moreover, this intention becomes a touchstone that you can return to in moments of doubt or difficulty. When the path to forgiveness feels arduous, your journal serves as a reminder of why you embarked on this journey in the first place. It reinforces your commitment to healing and provides the strength to persevere.

So, use your journal as a sacred space to nurture and reaffirm your intention for forgiveness. With each entry, you're nurturing the seeds of healing, cultivating the soil of understanding, and paving the way for transformation.

Reflecting On Perspectives

Reflecting on perspectives is a profound exercise in your journey toward forgiveness and healing. In your journal, you have the opportunity to become both the narrator and the listener, the protagonist and the observer of your own story.

Start by articulating your perspective, emotions, and experiences surrounding the hurt. This self-expression is cathartic and essential for processing your feelings.

Next, challenge yourself to step into the shoes of others involved. Write from their perspectives to understand their motivations, fears, and vulnerabilities. This exercise fosters empathy and compassion, allowing you to see the situation's complexities through different lenses.

As you navigate these diverse viewpoints within the pages of your journal, you'll gain a more comprehensive understanding of the situation. This expanded awareness can be a catalyst for forgiveness. It doesn't mean condoning harmful actions; rather, it's about acknowledging the humanity of all parties involved.

Ultimately, journaling provides a safe and supportive space to explore the multifaceted dimensions of forgiveness. It allows you to reflect, empathize, and gradually open your heart to the possibility of letting go of resentment and finding peace.

Creating A Journaling Ritual

Life can get busy, and finding time for yourself may seem challenging. However, carving out a few moments each day for journaling can make a difference. Consider integrating journaling into your daily routine – during your morning coffee, bedtime, or lunch break. It doesn't need to be a lengthy session; a few minutes of reflection can be incredibly impactful.

Journaling Amidst A Busy Schedule

While your schedule may be demanding, remember that self-care is a priority. Journaling can be a simple endeavor. Keep a small notebook or journal ready to capture your thoughts whenever a spare moment arises. Whether it's jotting down a few sentences, phrases, or even just emotions, these snippets can gradually accumulate into a meaningful healing journey.

Patience And Self-Compassion

As you navigate this forgiveness journey through journaling, remember that healing takes time. Be patient with yourself and allow the process to unfold organically. There's no rush to forgiveness; it's a personal journey that unfolds in its own time. Cultivate self-compassion, acknowledging that you're taking necessary steps towards your well-being.

Dear [Name], journaling can be your refuge during pain, guiding you toward forgiveness and healing. Trust in your ability to heal, and embrace journaling as a powerful tool to assist you on this transformative journey.

Journal On A Busy Schedule

Being intentional with journaling is like setting a compass to navigate the vast landscape of your inner world. It's a purposeful commitment to self-discovery, growth, and well-being. Here's why and how to be intentional with your journaling practice:

Clarify Your Purpose

Before you begin journaling, take a moment to clarify your purpose. Ask yourself why you're journaling. Is it to gain insights into your emotions, track your progress, or explore specific themes in your life? Each journaling session becomes more focused and meaningful when you have a clear purpose.

Set Specific Goals

Intentionality thrives on specificity. Set specific goals for your journaling practice. For example, if you're working on personal growth, your goal might be identifying and challenging limiting beliefs. If you're journaling for emotional well-being, your goal could be to express and process difficult emotions. Having clear goals gives your journaling session direction.

Choose The Right Time

Be intentional about when you journal. Select a time that aligns with your energy levels and schedule. Some people find mornings ideal for reflection, while others prefer evenings. Consistency in timing helps establish a routine and ensures you prioritize journaling.

Create A Sacred Space

Designate a space where you can journal without distractions. It could be a cozy corner of your home or a peaceful outdoor spot. This sacred space signals to your mind that you're entering a zone of self-exploration and reflection.

Reflect And Review

Periodically review your journal entries. This allows you to track progress, notice patterns, and revisit your goals. Reflecting on your journal can also be a powerful tool for personal growth, as it helps you connect the dots and gain deeper insights into your life.

Experiment With Different Techniques

Journaling isn't one-size-fits-all. Be intentional about experimenting with various journaling techniques. Try prompts, free-writing, gratitude journaling, or even art journaling. Find what resonates with you and supports your intentions.

Stay Committed

Consistency is key. Make a commitment to journal regularly, even if it's just for a few minutes each day. Intentional journaling is most effective when it becomes a habit. Set reminders if needed to ensure you stick to your practice.

Being intentional with journaling transforms it from a mere habit into a powerful tool for self-discovery and growth. It empowers you to explore your inner world with purpose and clarity, helping you make meaningful strides in your journey.

Remember, journaling is a flexible practice that can adapt to your schedule. The key is consistency, even if it's just a few minutes a day. Over time, these small moments of reflection can significantly impact your well-being and personal growth.

Forgiving Hidden Addictions

Forgiveness Reflection of the Day

Dear Me,

As I journey through the healing waves, I confront the shadows cast by the hidden addictions that have left their mark on my family. In the realm of forgiveness, I extend my compassion to those who struggled with these secrets and myself.

I forgive myself for not recognizing the signs earlier or understanding the depths of their struggles. Just as I extend grace to others, I embrace it for myself. I release the burden of blame that I've carried and replace it with understanding.

As I navigate this healing path, I acknowledge that the pain caused by hidden addictions cannot define my worth or future. While these secrets have cast a shadow, they do not dictate the entirety of my story. Through forgiveness, I release the weight that these addictions have placed upon my shoulders.

I choose to forgive those who kept these secrets hidden. I understand that the shame and fear that drove them to conceal their struggles were powerful adversaries.

As I am on a healing journey, I acknowledge that they are battling their demons.

In embracing forgiveness, I pave the way for my healing. I acknowledge that the scars left by hidden addictions do not have to be permanent. I have the power to rise above, to shed the shadows, and to craft a future that is not tethered to the past.

Healing is not linear; it's a journey filled with twists, turns, and moments of self-discovery. I permit myself to feel various emotions – anger, sadness, confusion – while still moving towards forgiveness. Each step I take is a stride towards reclaiming my power and sense of self.

As I close this reflection, I affirm that the secrets of the past do not define me. My resilience, capacity for growth, and unwavering commitment to healing represent me. Through forgiveness, I pave the way for a brighter future, one where the shadows of hidden addictions no longer cast their darkness.

With compassion and determination,

[Your Name]

Meditative Thought of the Day

Amidst the storm of secrets, I embark on a journey of healing. I recognize that healing starts with self-forgiveness. Just as I extend grace to others, I embrace it for myself, releasing the weight of guilt and shame that kept me captive.

Deeper Connection Within

1. How can you create a safe and nurturing space for yourself to process the pain and emotions that have emerged?

_____

_____

_____

_____

_____

_____

2. What does forgiveness mean to you, and how do you imagine it could transform your healing journey?

_____

_____

_____

_____

_____

_____

3. How can you extend compassion toward yourself as you navigate this challenging process?

_____

_____

_____

_____

_____

_____

Loving Statements About Me

I am rewriting my family's legacy with strength and resilience.

I release the weight of family secrets and step into my light.

I have the power to transform my pain into purpose.

Gratitude Reflection of the Day

Today, I am profoundly grateful for the healing journey that has allowed me to break the cycle of generational wounds, creating a brighter path for future generations.

Inner Reflections

Forgiveness For Revenge Affairs And Long-Term Affairs

Forgiveness Reflection of the Day

Dear Me,

In the realm of healing, I confront the weight of family secrets born from affairs that have left their mark on our lives. Through the transformative power of forgiveness, I extend compassion to those involved and myself.

I forgive myself for the moments of doubt and confusion that clouded my perception. Just as I offer understanding to others, I turn that empathy inward. I release the burden of self-blame and replace it with the gentle reminder that I deserve grace.

As I navigate this path toward healing, I understand that the pain caused by affairs does not define my worth or destiny. While these secrets have caused turmoil, they do not determine the entirety of my story. Through forgiveness, I release these affairs' hold on my emotions.

I choose to forgive those who were involved in these affairs. I acknowledge that their actions were borne from complex emotions and circumstances. I extend that same understanding to them as I seek knowledge for myself.

Forgiveness is not a singular act; it's a continuous journey. It's about acknowledging my emotions, processing them, and then releasing their grip on my heart. Each step I take towards forgiveness is personal empowerment and emotional liberation.

Through forgiveness, I carve a path towards healing and transformation. I embrace the idea that these affairs do not have to dictate my happiness or my future. My worth is not tied to the actions of others; it is rooted in my capacity to heal and grow.

As I pen this letter, I declare that I am more than the secrets that have haunted our family. I am a force of resilience, growth, and unwavering determination. Through forgiveness, I free myself from the chains of the past and step boldly into a future shaped by my own choices.

With compassion and strength,

[Your Name]

Meditative Thought of the Day

In the space of forgiveness, I find my strength. The secrets I've uncovered and those I've held no longer define me. I reclaim my power through forgiveness, acknowledging that I am not a prisoner of the past.

Deeper Connection Within

1. What forms of support do you believe would be most beneficial as you take steps toward healing and growth?

_____

_____

_____

_____

_____

_____

2. What small steps have you taken to initiate your healing journey?

_____

_____

_____

_____

_____

_____

3. How might cultivating self-love and self-acceptance affect your ability to forgive and heal?

_____

_____

_____

_____

_____

_____

Loving Statements About Me

I choose to forgive, not for them, but for my peace and growth.

I am building a new story of empowerment and authenticity.

I have the strength to break free from the chains of the past.

Gratitude Reflection of the Day

I appreciate the strength and courage it took to welcome forgiveness into my heart, releasing the burdens of resentment and pain.

Inner Reflections

Forgiveness For Secret Marriages

Forgiveness Reflection of the Day

Dear Me,

Amid the echoes of hidden marriages and their far-reaching impact, I embark on a healing journey. Through the power of forgiveness, I extend compassion not only to those who were involved in these hidden unions but also to myself.

I forgive myself for the moments of confusion and disbelief that clouded my understanding. Just as I offer empathy to others, I direct that understanding inward. I release the weight of self-blame and replace it with the gentle recognition that I, too, deserve grace.

As I navigate this path toward healing, I acknowledge that the shockwaves of hidden marriages do not define my essence or destiny. While these secrets have caused upheaval, they do not dominate my narrative. Through forgiveness, I unburden myself from the emotional toll of these revelations.

I choose to forgive those who concealed these marriages. I understand a complex interplay of emotions and circumstances drove their choices.

As I strive for comprehension, I extend that same understanding to them.

Forgiveness is a process, one that involves acknowledging my emotions, confronting them, and ultimately choosing to release their grip on my heart. Each step towards forgiveness brings me closer to personal empowerment and emotional liberation.

Through forgiveness, I forge a path towards healing and transformation. I embrace the notion that hidden marriages need not cast a shadow over my happiness or my future. My worth transcends the actions of others; it's rooted in my resilience and capacity to heal.

As I pen this letter, I declare that I am more than the tumultuous secrets that have shaken our family. I am a vessel of strength, growth, and unwavering determination. Through forgiveness, I break free from the chains of the past and stride boldly into a future crafted by my own choices.

With compassion and resilience,

[Your Name]

Meditative Thought of the Day

As I navigate this new terrain, I recognize the importance of setting boundaries. These boundaries are not walls but expressions of self-love and self-care. They create a safe space where my healing journey can thrive.

Deeper Connection Within

1. What does the word "forgiveness" evoke in you, and how can you redefine it to align with your needs?

_____

_____

_____

_____

_____

_____

2. How can you honor your emotions while opening the door to the possibility of forgiveness?

_____

_____

_____

_____

_____

_____

3. What role does your inner strength play in your ability to face this challenge and work toward healing?

_____

_____

_____

_____

_____

_____

Loving Statements About Me

My worth is not defined by the secrets that once held me back.

I am rewriting my narrative with courage and determination.

I embrace the power of forgiveness as a key to my healing.

Gratitude Reflection of the Day

I'm thankful for the mental freedom from releasing the past, allowing me to live in the present moment with clarity and purpose.

Inner Reflections

Forgiveness For Secret Children

Forgiveness Reflection of the Day

Dear Me,

As I tread the path of healing in the wake of hidden secret children, I confront the weight of these revelations that have shaken the very foundations of our family. Through the profound act of forgiveness, I extend compassion to the secret children themselves and the family that unknowingly harbored these secrets.

I forgive myself for the moments of shock and disbelief that clouded my understanding. Just as I offer understanding to others, I direct that empathy inward. I release the weight of self-blame and replace it with the gentle reminder that I deserve forgiveness and grace.

Navigating this healing journey, I understand that discovering hidden secret children does not define my worth or the essence of our family. While these revelations have caused upheaval, they need not dictate the entirety of our story. Through forgiveness, I liberate myself from the emotional toll of these secrets.

I forgive those who concealed these truths, recognizing that many complex emotions and circumstances drove their actions. As I strive to understand within myself, I extend that understanding to them.

Forgiveness is an ongoing process that involves acknowledging my emotions, confronting them, and ultimately releasing their hold on my heart. Each step towards forgiveness is a step towards empowerment and emotional liberation.

Through forgiveness, I create a path towards healing and transformation. I embrace the notion that the presence of secret children need not cast a permanent shadow over our family. Our worth transcends the actions of the past; it's rooted in our resilience and ability to heal.

As I pen this reflection, I declare that I am more than the shocking revelations that have jolted our family. I am a vessel of strength, growth, and unwavering determination. Through forgiveness, I release myself from the chains of the past and march confidently into a future shaped by my choices.

With compassion and strength,

[Your Name]

Meditative Thought of the Day

Embracing Vulnerability, Cultivating Resilience

Vulnerability has become my wellspring of resilience. By acknowledging my pain and confronting my secrets, I open the door to authentic growth. Through vulnerability, I find the courage to heal.

Deeper Connection Within

1. How do you envision the healing process impacting yourself and your family dynamic?

_____

_____

_____

_____

_____

_____

2. What might be the first step you can take to initiate an internal shift towards forgiveness?

_____

_____

_____

_____

_____

_____

3. How can you release the pain and resentment associated with the family secrets and begin to heal?

_____

_____

_____

_____

_____

_____

Loving Statements About Me

I am deserving of love, understanding, and happiness.

I am resilient, and I can overcome any obstacle in my path.

I am the author of my story and choose to make it extraordinary.

Gratitude Reflection of the Day

I express gratitude for my profound transformation, knowing that my healing ripples outward, touching the lives of those I love.

Inner Reflections

Forgiveness For Incest

Forgiveness Reflection of the Day

Dear Me,

In the realm of healing from family secrets marred by the inappropriate behavior of a family member, I embark on a journey of forgiveness. Through this transformative act, I extend compassion to those who hid the truth and myself as I navigate the intricate web of surfaced emotions.

I forgive myself for moments of confusion and self-blame that clouded my understanding. Just as I extend empathy to others, I direct that same empathy inward. I release the grip of self-condemnation and replace it with the knowledge that I, too, deserve healing and grace.

As I traverse this path of healing, I recognize that the veil of secrecy surrounding inappropriate behavior does not define my worth or the essence of our family. While these hidden truths have cast shadows, they need not dictate the entirety of our story. Through forgiveness, I release the emotional burden they have placed upon me.

I forgive those who chose to keep the secret of inappropriate behavior, acknowledging the complex emotions and circumstances that influenced their decisions. As I strive to understand within myself, I extend that understanding to them.

Forgiveness is confronting my emotions, facing them head-on, and ultimately releasing their grip on my heart. Each step towards forgiveness signifies a step towards personal empowerment and emotional liberation.

Through forgiveness, I create room for healing and transformation. The darkness of inappropriate behavior does not have to cast shadows over our family forever. My worth transcends the actions of others; it's rooted in my strength and capacity to heal.

As I write this reflection, I affirm that I am more than the pain caused by the family secrets surrounding inappropriate behavior. I am a vessel of resilience, growth, and unwavering determination. Through forgiveness, I liberate myself from the chains of the past and stride confidently into a future shaped by my choices.

With compassion and strength,

[Your Name]

Meditative Thought of the Day

In the realm of healing, self-forgiveness becomes my guiding light. I release the grip of self-blame and recognize that I, too, deserve compassion. Through self-forgiveness, I unlock the door to liberation.

Deeper Connection Within

1. What qualities of forgiveness resonate with you and can guide your journey toward growth?

_____

_____

_____

_____

_____

_____

2. How can you connect with your values and principles to guide your healing process?

_____

_____

_____

_____

_____

_____

3. How might sharing your feelings and perspectives with a trusted friend or therapist support your growth?

_____

_____

_____

_____

_____

_____

Loving Statements About Me

My past does not define me; I have the power to shape my future.

I release the pain of the past and welcome a new era of growth.

I am stronger than the secrets that once haunted me.

Gratitude Reflection of the Day

Today, I celebrate the inner peace that comes from letting go of the emotional baggage I carried from the past, freeing my spirit to soar.

Inner Reflections

Forgiveness For Secret Health Conditions

Forgiveness Reflection of the Day

Dear Me,

As I tread the path of healing after a family member's hidden health condition, I grapple with the pain and devastation caused by this secret, especially concerning a terminal illness. Through the power of forgiveness, I extend compassion to those who kept the secret and myself as I navigate the complex emotions it has stirred.

I forgive myself for the moments of shock and disbelief that clouded my understanding. Just as I extend empathy to others, I direct that empathy inward. I release the weight of self-blame and replace it with the gentle reminder that I deserve healing and grace.

In this healing journey, I understand that the anguish of hidden health conditions, especially terminal ones, does not define my worth or the essence of our family. While this revelation has left us reeling, it need not determine the entirety of our story. Through forgiveness, I release the emotional burden that this secret has placed upon my heart.

I forgive those withheld this information, recognizing that a complex interplay of emotions and circumstances drove their actions. As I seek understanding within myself, I extend that understanding to them.

Forgiveness is an ongoing process that involves acknowledging my emotions, confronting them, and ultimately deciding to release their grip on my heart. Each step towards forgiveness signifies a step towards personal empowerment and emotional liberation.

Through forgiveness, I pave the way for healing and transformation. I embrace the belief that the shadow of this secret health condition, even if terminal, does not have to cast a permanent darkness over our family. My worth transcends the actions of others; it is rooted in my strength and capacity to heal.

As I pen this letter, I declare that I am more than the pain caused by the secret health condition that has shaken our family. I am a vessel of resilience, growth, and unwavering determination. Through forgiveness, I break free from the chains of the past and move boldly into a future shaped by my own choices.

With compassion and strength,

[Your Name]

Meditative Thought of the Day

As the landscape shifts, I navigate towards a new normal. Setting boundaries is my compass, guiding me toward relationships that uplift and nurture. I shape this new chapter with intention and purpose.

Deeper Connection Within

1. What would it feel like to free yourself from the weight of carrying this burden and embrace healing?

_____

_____

_____

_____

_____

_____

2. How can you create a sense of personal empowerment even within the struggle for forgiveness?

_____

_____

_____

_____

_____

_____

3. How might viewing forgiveness as a journey rather than an endpoint help alleviate pressure?

_____

_____

_____

_____

_____

_____

Loving Statements About Me

I forgive, not to forget, but to reclaim my peace of mind.

I am reclaiming my power and rewriting my destiny.

I am building a legacy of strength, compassion, and authenticity.

Gratitude Reflection of the Day

I am grateful for the understanding and empathy that have grown within me, fostering deeper connections with others who have also experienced generational wounds.

Inner Reflections

Forgiveness For Domestic Violence

Forgiveness Reflection of the Day

Dear Me,

Amid the echoes of domestic violence, compounded by the weight of family secrecy, I embark on a healing journey. Through the power of forgiveness, I extend compassion to those who perpetuated this cycle and myself as I navigate the complex web of emotions it has woven.

I forgive myself for the moments of confusion and guilt that clouded my understanding. Just as I extend empathy to others, I direct that empathy inward. I release the burden of self-blame and replace it with the knowledge that I, too, deserve healing and grace.

In the process of healing, I realize that the trauma of domestic violence and the betrayal of family secrecy do not define my worth or the essence of our family. While these painful experiences have left scars, they need not dictate the entirety of our story. Through forgiveness, I release the emotional toll they have taken.

I forgive those who enabled the secrecy, recognizing that complex emotions and circumstances influenced their actions. Just as I strive for understanding within myself, I extend that same understanding to them.

Forgiveness is a journey that entails acknowledging my emotions, confronting them head-on, and ultimately choosing to release their grip on my heart. Every step toward forgiveness signifies a step toward personal empowerment and emotional liberation.

Through forgiveness, I pave the way for healing and transformation. I believe the darkness of domestic violence and family secrecy need not define my future. My worth surpasses the actions of others; it's rooted in my strength and capacity to heal.

As I pen this letter, I declare that I am more than the pain caused by domestic violence and the secrecy that ensued. I am a beacon of resilience, growth, and unwavering determination. Through forgiveness, I cast off the chains of the past and stride confidently into a future shaped by my choices.

With compassion and strength,

[Your Name]

Meditative Thought of the Day

I choose to heal unconditionally. The absence of an apology doesn't hinder my journey; it empowers it. My healing is not contingent on external validation; it's a testament to my strength and resolve.

Deeper Connection Within

1. What practices or rituals can you integrate into your routine to promote healing and self-care?

_____

_____

_____

_____

_____

_____

2. How can you balance acknowledging the pain and nurturing hope for a brighter future?

_____

_____

_____

_____

_____

_____

3. What positive qualities or strengths can you draw from within yourself to aid your healing?

_____

_____

_____

_____

_____

_____

Loving Statements About Me

I release the grip of family secrets and open my heart to healing.

I am worthy of joy, love, and all life's blessings.

I choose to believe in my worth and potential.

Gratitude Reflection of the Day

I appreciate the forgiveness I've extended to myself for any past mistakes or missteps, recognizing that self-compassion is a key to healing.

Inner Reflections

Forgiveness For Stolen Children

Forgiveness Reflection of the Day

Dear Me,

While grappling with the heart-wrenching pain of stolen children and the shroud of family secrets, I embark on a healing journey. Through the power of forgiveness, I extend compassion to those who orchestrated these actions and myself as I navigate the intricate web of emotions they have stirred.

I forgive myself for the moments of confusion and grief that clouded my understanding. Just as I extend empathy to others, I direct that same empathy inward. I release the burden of self-blame and replace it with the knowledge that I, too, deserve healing and grace.

As I navigate this healing path, I acknowledge that the trauma of stolen children and the weight of family secrets do not define my worth or the essence of our family. While these painful experiences have cast a shadow, they do not have to dictate the entirety of our story. Through forgiveness, I release the emotional toll they have taken.

I forgive those who orchestrated these actions, recognizing the multifaceted emotions and circumstances that led to their choices. As I seek understanding within myself, I extend that understanding to them.

Forgiveness is acknowledging my emotions, confronting them head-on, and ultimately deciding to release their grip on my heart. Each step towards forgiveness signifies a step towards personal empowerment and emotional liberation.

Through forgiveness, I pave the way for healing and transformation. I embrace the belief that the darkness of stolen children and the veil of family secrets do not have to determine my future. My worth surpasses the actions of others; it is rooted in my strength and capacity to heal.

As I pen this letter, I declare that I am more than the pain caused by stolen children and the shrouded secrets that haunt us. I am a beacon of resilience, growth, and unwavering determination. Through forgiveness, I break free from the chains of the past and stride confidently into a future shaped by my choices.

With compassion and strength,

[Your Name]

Meditative Thought of the Day

While secrets may have entwined my story, they don't define me. I take ownership of my actions, acknowledging that I am the author of my narrative. Through accountability, I pave the way for growth.

Deeper Connection Within

1. How do you envision the process of forgiveness impacting your ability to create a new narrative for your life?

_____

_____

_____

_____

_____

_____

2. How can you cultivate resilience within yourself as you navigate this challenging terrain?

_____

_____

_____

_____

_____

_____

3. What insights might you gain from exploring the underlying motivations behind the family secrets?

_____

_____

_____

_____

_____

_____

Loving Statements About Me

I am breaking free from old patterns and embracing new possibilities.

I can create positive change in my life and the lives of others.

I am writing a story of resilience, forgiveness, and empowerment.

Gratitude Reflection of the Day

I'm thankful for the moments of clarity and insight that have illuminated my healing journey, guiding me toward greater self-awareness.

Inner Reflections

Forgiveness For Hiding A Rape Or Molestation

Forgiveness Reflection of the Day

Dear Me,

Amid the darkness of a family secret that concealed a heinous act of rape or molestation, I embark on a journey of healing that centers around the transformative power of forgiveness. Through this profound act, I extend compassion to those who chose to protect the predator and myself as I navigate the complex terrain of emotions this revelation has ignited.

I forgive myself for the moments of shock and disbelief that cast shadows on my understanding. Just as I extend empathy to others, I direct that empathy inward. I release the weight of self-blame and replace it with the gentle reminder that I deserve healing and grace.

As I navigate this path of healing, I recognize that the trauma inflicted by a family secret covering up such reprehensible acts does not define my worth or the essence of our family. While this revelation has left us reeling, it need not dictate the entirety of our story.

Through forgiveness, I release this secret's emotional burden upon me.

I forgive those who shielded the predator, acknowledging the complex interplay of emotions and circumstances that led to their actions. As I strive to understand within myself, I extend that understanding to them.

Forgiveness is acknowledging my emotions, facing them head-on, and ultimately deciding to release their grip on my heart. Each step towards forgiveness signifies a step towards personal empowerment and emotional liberation.

Through forgiveness, I pave the way for healing and transformation. The shadow of this secret act does not have to cast a permanent darkness over our family. My worth transcends the actions of others; it's rooted in my strength and capacity to heal.

As I write this reflection, I declare that I am more than the pain caused by the family secret that covered up an act of rape or molestation. I am a vessel of resilience, growth, and unwavering determination. Through forgiveness, I break free from the chains of the past and stride confidently into a future shaped by my own choices.

With compassion and strength,

[Your Name]

Meditative Thought of the Day

My life is a canvas of transformation. I paint my future with the brushstrokes of healing, forgiveness, and resilience. In every choice I make, I craft a masterpiece that defies the constraints of the past.

Deeper Connection Within

1. How can you embrace your healing journey while granting your family members the same opportunity?

_____
_____
_____
_____
_____
_____

2. How do you see forgiveness as a stepping stone toward personal freedom and authenticity?

_____
_____
_____
_____
_____
_____

3. What practices, hobbies, or passions bring you a sense of solace and can contribute to your healing?

_____
_____
_____
_____
_____
_____

Loving Statements About Me

The secrets no longer define me; my courage defines me.

I am worthy of forgiveness, both from others and from myself.

I have the power to shape my destiny and create a bright future.

Gratitude Reflection of the Day

Today, I honor the resilience of my spirit, which has allowed me to overcome challenges and emerge stronger and wiser.

Inner Reflections

Forgiveness For Secret Siblings

Forgiveness Reflection of the Day

Dear Me,

In the wake of discovering the hidden truths surrounding secret siblings—whether born of adoption, kept secret as a father's child, or hidden due to circumstances—my heart is heavy with mixed emotions. Through the journey of forgiveness, I extend compassion not only to those who harbored these secrets but also to myself as I navigate this intricate path of healing.

I forgive myself for the moments of shock and confusion that clouded my understanding. Just as I extend empathy to others, I direct that same empathy inward. I release the weight of self-blame and replace it with the knowledge that I, too, deserve healing and grace.

In this healing journey, I understand that the revelation of secret siblings, regardless of the circumstances, does not define my worth or the essence of our family. While these hidden truths may have caused turmoil, they need not dictate the entirety of our story. Through forgiveness, I release their emotional burden on my heart.

I forgive those who kept these secrets, recognizing that complex emotions and circumstances influenced their actions. As I seek understanding within myself, I extend that understanding to them.

Forgiveness is a path of acknowledging my emotions, facing them head-on, and ultimately releasing their grip on my heart. Each step towards forgiveness signifies a step towards personal empowerment and emotional liberation.

Through forgiveness, I clear the way for healing and transformation. The shadow of these secret siblings does not have to cast a permanent darkness over our family. My worth transcends the actions of others; it is rooted in my strength and capacity to heal.

As I put pen to paper, I declare that I am more than the revelations of secret siblings that have shaken our family's foundation. I am a vessel of resilience, growth, and unwavering determination. Through forgiveness, I cast off the chains of the past and move boldly into a future shaped by my choices.

With compassion and strength,

[Your Name]

Meditative Thought of the Day

Just as I let go of secrets, I release the shackles that held me captive. In the space created, healing blooms. The decisions of others do not limit me; I am boundless and ready to embrace my potential.

Deeper Connection Within

1. How might self-forgiveness for any judgments you've held about yourself due to these secrets be transformative?

_____

_____

_____

_____

_____

_____

2. What role does vulnerability play in your ability to express your emotions and work towards healing?

_____

_____

_____

_____

_____

3. How can you release the grip of the past and create space for new beginnings and positive change?

_____

_____

_____

_____

_____

Loving Statements About Me

I am the architect of my life and choose to build a strong foundation.

I am letting go of what no longer serves me and making room for growth.

I am rewriting my history with self-love, acceptance, and strength.

Gratitude Reflection of the Day

I express gratitude for the love and support of those who have walked beside me on this healing path, offering their compassion and understanding.

Inner Reflections

Forgiveness For Neglecting Family Members

Forgiveness Reflection of the Day

Dear Me,

While grappling with the wounds inflicted by family secrets—ones that led to the neglect or disregard of a family member—I embark on a journey of healing through forgiveness. Through this act of compassion, I extend understanding to those who made such choices and myself as I navigate the complexities of emotions that have arisen.

I forgive myself for the moments of confusion and pain that clouded my understanding. Just as I extend empathy to others, I direct that same empathy inward. I release the burden of self-blame and replace it with the knowledge that I, too, deserve healing and grace.

Amid this healing journey, I recognize that the impact of family secrets that led to neglect or disregard does not define my worth or the essence of our family. While these painful experiences have left scars, they do not have to determine the entirety of our story. Through forgiveness, I release the emotional toll they have taken.

I forgive those involved in these secrets, acknowledging the complex emotions and circumstances that influenced their decisions. As I seek understanding within myself, I extend that understanding to them.

Forgiveness is a path of acknowledging my emotions, facing them head-on, and ultimately releasing their grip on my heart. Each step toward forgiveness signifies a step toward personal empowerment and emotional liberation.

Through forgiveness, I open the door for healing and transformation. I embrace the belief that the shadows cast by these family secrets do not have to define my future. My worth surpasses the actions of others; it's rooted in my strength and capacity to heal.

As I write this letter, I affirm that I am more than the pain caused by the family secrets that led to neglect or disregard. I am a beacon of resilience, growth, and unwavering determination. Through forgiveness, I break free from the chains of the past and stride confidently into a future shaped by my choices.

With compassion and strength,

[Your Name]

Meditative Thought of the Day

The tapestry of my worth is woven with threads of resilience and self-love. I am deserving of healing, grace, and forgiveness. I stand tall, honoring my intrinsic value, independent of external judgments.

Deeper Connection Within

1. What could be gained from opening a dialogue with family members about the impact of these secrets?

_____

_____

_____

_____

_____

_____

2. How can you embrace the journey of forgiveness without necessarily needing to forget or condone the actions?

_____

_____

_____

_____

_____

_____

3. What insights can you gain from looking at your family members as complex individuals shaped by their experiences?

_____

_____

_____

_____

_____

_____

Loving Statements About Me

I am resilient and rise above the challenges that come my way.

I am releasing the pain of the past and embracing a future filled with possibilities.

I am rewriting my story with authenticity, courage, and grace.

Gratitude Reflection of the Day

I'm thankful for the newfound sense of empowerment that comes from breaking free from generational patterns and creating my destiny.

Inner Reflections

Forgiveness For Hiding Gender Identity And Sexual Orientation

Forgiveness Reflection of the Day

Dear Me,

As I stand at the crossroads of unveiling the family secret that concealed my true sexual orientation or gender identity, I embark on a journey of healing and forgiveness. Through this profound act, I extend compassion to those who chose to hide this truth and myself as I navigate the intricate web of emotions it has stirred.

I forgive myself for the moments of confusion and self-doubt that clouded my understanding. Just as I extend empathy to others, I direct that same empathy inward. I release the burden of self-blame and replace it with the knowledge that I, too, deserve healing and grace.

In the healing process, I realized that the secrecy that shrouded my true self does not define my worth or the essence of our family. While these hidden truths have caused pain, they need not dictate the entirety of our story. Through forgiveness, I release the emotional weight they have placed upon me.

I forgive those who chose to hide my sexual orientation or gender identity, recognizing the complexities of emotions and circumstances that led to their choices. As I strive to understand within myself, I extend that understanding to them.

Forgiveness is acknowledging my emotions, confronting them head-on, and ultimately deciding to release their grip on my heart. Each step towards forgiveness signifies a step towards personal empowerment and emotional liberation.

Through forgiveness, I pave the way for healing and transformation. I embrace the belief that the shadows of secrecy around my sexual orientation or gender identity do not have to cast a permanent darkness over our family. My worth transcends the actions of others; it's rooted in my strength and capacity to heal.

As I write this reflection, I affirm that I am more than the pain caused by the family secrets that hid my true self. I am a beacon of resilience, growth, and unwavering determination. Through forgiveness, I break free from the chains of the past and stride confidently into a future shaped by my choices.

With compassion and strength,

[Your Name]

Meditative Thought of the Day

As I set boundaries, I gift myself protection and honor. These boundaries remind me of my worth, creating a safe haven for healing and relationships.

Deeper Connection Within

1. How might focusing on the present moment help alleviate the weight of past grievances?

_____

_____

_____

_____

_____

_____

2. How can you honor your journey by recognizing that healing takes time and patience?

_____

_____

_____

_____

_____

_____

3. What would it look like to set small intentions for healing each day, regardless of the struggles?

_____

_____

_____

_____

_____

_____

Loving Statements About Me

I am a survivor, and my strength shines brighter than any family secret.

I am stepping into my power and embracing my unique greatness.

I forgive myself for any judgments I held against myself due to family secrets.

Gratitude Reflection of the Day

I appreciate the opportunities for growth and transformation that have arisen from my commitment to healing generational wounds.

Inner Reflections

Forgiveness For Undisclosed Adoption

Forgiveness Reflection of the Day

Dear Me,

Amidst the veil of family secrets that hid the truth of my undisclosed adoption, I embarked on a journey of healing and forgiveness. Through this profound act, I extend compassion to those who chose to keep this truth hidden and to myself as I navigate the complex web of emotions that have arisen.

I forgive myself for the moments of confusion and self-doubt that clouded my understanding. Just as I extend empathy to others, I direct that same empathy inward. I release the weight of self-blame and replace it with the knowledge that I, too, deserve healing and grace.

In the healing process, I recognize that the shroud of secrecy around my undisclosed adoption does not define my worth or the essence of our family. While this hidden truth has caused ripples of pain, it need not dictate the entirety of our story. Through forgiveness, I release the emotional burden it has placed upon me.

I forgive those who chose to keep my adoption a secret, acknowledging the complex emotions and circumstances that led to their decision. As I strive to understand within myself, I extend that understanding to them.

Forgiveness is acknowledging my emotions, facing them head-on, and ultimately deciding to release their grip on my heart. Each step towards forgiveness signifies a step towards personal empowerment and emotional liberation.

Through forgiveness, I clear the path for healing and transformation. I believe the veil of secrecy around my undisclosed adoption does not have to cast a permanent shadow over our family. My worth transcends the actions of others; it's rooted in my strength and capacity to heal.

As I pen this reflection, I declare that I am more than the pain caused by the family secret that concealed adoption. I am a vessel of resilience, growth, and unwavering determination. Through forgiveness, I break free from the chains of the past and stride confidently into a future shaped by my choices.

With compassion and strength,

[Your Name]

Meditative Thought of the Day

In the face of challenges, I am a flower blooming through cracks in the pavement. I persevere, drawing strength from within. The adversity I face only nourishes my growth.

Deeper Connection Within

1. How can you redefine your self-worth beyond the influence of these family secrets?

_____

_____

_____

_____

_____

_____

2. What steps can you take to cultivate a sense of agency and control within your healing process?

_____

_____

_____

_____

_____

_____

3. How might your experiences help you connect with and empathize with others facing similar struggles?

_____

_____

_____

_____

_____

_____

Loving Statements About Me

I am embracing my worthiness and allowing love to flow into my life.

I am releasing the burden of the past and stepping into my authentic self.

I am rewriting the script of my life with positivity and determination.

Gratitude Reflection of the Day

Today, I celebrate the release of old traumas and grievances, making space for love, joy, and inner peace.

Inner Reflections

Forgiveness For Hiding Mental Health Disorders

Forgiveness Reflection of the Day

Dear Me,

In the realm of family secrets that concealed the truth of mental health disorders, I embarked on a journey of healing and forgiveness. Through this transformative act, I extend compassion to those who chose to keep these truths hidden and to myself as I navigate the intricate tapestry of emotions that have surfaced.

I forgive myself for moments of confusion and self-blame that clouded my understanding. Just as I extend empathy to others, I direct that same empathy inward. I release the burden of self-condemnation and replace it with the understanding that I, too, deserve healing and grace.

As I embark on this journey, I acknowledge that the shroud of secrecy surrounding mental health disorders does not define my worth or the essence of our family. While these hidden truths have cast shadows, they need not dictate the entirety of our story. Through forgiveness, I release the emotional weight they have placed upon me.

I forgive those who concealed mental health disorders, recognizing the complexity of emotions and circumstances that influenced their decisions. As I strive to understand within myself, I extend that understanding to them.

Forgiveness is a path of confronting my emotions, facing them head-on, and ultimately releasing their grip on my heart. Each step towards forgiveness signifies a step towards personal empowerment and emotional liberation.

Through forgiveness, I pave the way for healing and transformation. The veil of secrecy around mental health disorders does not have to cast a permanent shadow over our family. My worth transcends the actions of others; it's rooted in my strength and capacity to heal.

As I write this reflection, I affirm that I am more than the pain caused by the family secrets that concealed mental health disorders. I am a vessel of resilience, growth, and unwavering determination. Through forgiveness, I break free from the chains of the past and stride confidently into a future shaped by my choices.

With compassion and strength,

[Your Name]

Meditative Thought of the Day

Self-forgiveness is not an admission of wrongdoing; it's a liberating act of compassion. As I forgive myself for keeping secrets, I free myself from the chains of self-condemnation.

Deeper Connection Within

1. How do you envision your life when you can heal and grow beyond the influence of these secrets?

_____

_____

_____

_____

_____

_____

2. What opportunities might arise from embracing and using this challenge to fuel your personal development?

_____

_____

_____

_____

_____

_____

3. How can you create rituals that release negative energy and invite positivity?

_____

_____

_____

_____

_____

_____

Loving Statements About Me

I am building a legacy of love, healing, and resilience for future generations.

I am letting go of old stories and embracing a new empowerment narrative.

I am worthy of happiness, success, and fulfillment despite the past.

Gratitude Reflection of the Day

I am grateful for the mental clarity and emotional stability that healing has brought into my life.

Inner Reflections

Forgiveness For Exploiting Vulnerable Family Members

Forgiveness Reflection of the Day

Dear Me,

As I navigate the intricate terrain of family secrets that exploit vulnerable family members for personal gain or exclusion from inheritance, I embark on a journey of healing and forgiveness. Through this profound act, I extend compassion to those who chose to exploit and myself as I navigate the web of emotions that have surfaced.

I forgive myself for moments of confusion and self-blame that clouded my understanding. Just as I extend empathy to others, I direct that same empathy inward. I release the weight of self-condemnation and replace it with the understanding that I, too, deserve healing and grace.

In the healing process, I recognize that the veil of secrecy surrounding exploiting vulnerable family members does not define my worth or the essence of our family. While these hidden truths have caused pain, they need not dictate the entirety of our story. Through forgiveness, I release the emotional weight they have placed upon me.

I forgive those who chose to exploit vulnerable family members, recognizing the complexity of emotions and circumstances that influenced their decisions. As I strive to understand within myself, I extend that understanding to them.

Forgiveness is confronting my emotions, facing them head-on, and ultimately deciding to release their grip on my heart. Each step towards forgiveness signifies a step towards personal empowerment and emotional liberation.

Through forgiveness, I create a space for healing and transformation. The darkness of exploitation does not have to shadow our family permanently. My worth transcends the actions of others; it's rooted in my strength and capacity to heal.

As I write this reflection, I affirm that I am more than the pain caused by the family secrets that exploited vulnerable family members. I am a vessel of resilience, growth, and unwavering determination. Through forgiveness, I break free from the chains of the past and stride confidently into a future shaped by my choices.

With compassion and strength,

[Your Name]

Meditative Thought of the Day

Healing is my birthright, and I claim it without hesitation. The wounds of secrets and revelations don't define me. I am free to choose healing, renewal, and transformation.

Deeper Connection Within

1. How might your ability to forgive impact your own well-being and mental health?

---

2. What role does self-compassion play in your ability to heal and grow forward?

---

3. How can you harness your inner strength to overcome challenges and continue moving forward?

Loving Statements About Me

I am empowered to break the cycle and create a new path.

I am capable of healing and transforming any pain into strength.

I am reclaiming my power and stepping into my authentic purpose.

Gratitude Reflection of the Day

I express gratitude for the newfound sense of purpose and direction that has emerged due to my healing journey.

Inner Reflections

Forgiving Myself For Hiding A Family Secret

Forgiveness Reflection of the Day

Dear Me,

Standing at the intersection of my inner truth and the family secret I have chosen to hide, I embark on a journey of healing and forgiveness. Through this profound act, I extend compassion to myself and the intricate emotions that have led me to keep this hidden truth.

I forgive myself for moments of inner turmoil and the weight of guilt accompanying my decision to hide a devastating family secret. Just as I strive to understand others, I direct that understanding inward. I release the grip of self-judgment and replace it with the knowledge that I, too, deserve healing and grace.

In the healing process, I acknowledge that my decision to hide a family secret does not define my worth or essence. While this hidden truth has cast shadows over my heart, it need not dictate the entirety of my story. Through forgiveness, I release the emotional burden it has placed upon me.

I forgive myself for keeping a devastating family secret, acknowledging the complexity of emotions and circumstances that led to my choice. Just as I strive to extend understanding to others, I extend that same understanding to myself.

Forgiveness is a journey of facing my emotions, acknowledging them, and ultimately deciding to release their hold on my heart. Each step towards forgiveness marks a stride towards personal empowerment and emotional liberation.

Through forgiveness, I clear the path for healing and transformation. I embrace the belief that my decision to hide a family secret does not have to overshadow my existence forever. My worth transcends my actions, rooted in my capacity to heal and grow.

As I put pen to paper, I affirm that I am more than the decision I made to hide a devastating family secret. I am a beacon of resilience, growth, and unwavering determination. Through forgiveness, I free myself from the chains of the past and move forward into a future shaped by my choices.

With compassion and strength,

[Your Name]

Meditative Thought of the Day

I find my path to healing in the depths of discovery and vulnerability. I acknowledge the weight of the secrets I've uncovered and the hidden ones I've held. Just as I desire grace and forgiveness for others, I extend the same to myself. Through self-forgiveness, I unlock the door to liberation.

Boundaries become my guardians, shielding me as I navigate this new terrain. In the realm of the unknown, I embrace the power to shape my interactions and protect my heart. These boundaries are not barriers but expressions of self-love and respect.

I choose to heal unconditionally. The absence of an apology doesn't define my journey; it empowers it. My worth isn't anchored to the past but to my choices today. I release the shackles of the past, acknowledging that my healing journey is a personal endeavor disconnected from external validation.

In the tapestry of life, I recognize that my story is a mosaic of decisions, experiences, and emotions. While family secrets may be part of my narrative, they don't define me. I take accountability for my actions, acknowledging that I'm the steward of my choices and responsible for my growth.

I am a vessel of resilience, and within me resides the potential for transformation. As I walk this healing path, I carry the lantern of self-forgiveness, illuminating the way to a brighter future. I embrace the process of self-discovery, allowing it to shape me into the person I aspire to be.

In this journey, I find strength in vulnerability, grace in forgiveness, and power in setting boundaries. I am not merely a bystander to my story; I am its author. With unwavering determination, I heal, grow, and shape my destiny.

Today, I choose to release the grip of secrets, the burden of guilt, and the weight of unmet expectations. I navigate this path with a heart unburdened, a spirit uplifted, and a commitment to nurturing my well-being. I am resilient, I am worthy, and I am embracing healing amidst secrets.

Deeper Connection Within

1. How can you experience both the pain and the possibility of healing simultaneously?

_____

_____

_____

_____

_____

_____

2. What practices can help you tune into your inner wisdom and authentically navigate this journey?

_____

_____

_____

_____

_____

_____

3. How might acknowledging your feelings while embracing forgiveness contribute to your sense of freedom?

_____

_____

_____

_____

_____

_____

Loving Statements About Me

I am rewriting the narrative of my life with unwavering self-belief.

I am releasing the past and embracing a future of endless possibilities.

I am creating a legacy of love, compassion, and authenticity.

Gratitude Reflection of the Day

I'm thankful for the courage it took to confront the wounds of the past, knowing that true healing requires facing the darkness with an open heart.

Inner Reflections

Forgiveness For Adultery With Friends

Forgiveness Reflection of the Day

Dear Me,

As I navigate the intricate terrain of family secrets that involved adultery with a family friend, I embark on a journey of healing and forgiveness. Through this profound act, I extend compassion to those involved and myself as I navigate the surface web of emotions.

I forgive myself for moments of confusion and self-blame that clouded my understanding. Just as I extend empathy to others, I direct that same empathy inward. I release the weight of self-condemnation and replace it with the understanding that I, too, deserve healing and grace.

In the healing process, I recognize that the veil of secrecy surrounding adultery committed with a family friend does not define my worth or the essence of our family. While this hidden truth has cast shadows, it need not dictate the entirety of our story. Through forgiveness, I release the emotional weight they have placed upon me.

I forgive those involved in the adultery, recognizing the complex emotions and circumstances that influenced their decisions. As I strive to understand within myself, I extend that understanding to them.

Forgiveness is confronting my emotions, facing them head-on, and ultimately releasing their grip on my heart. Each step towards forgiveness signifies a step towards personal empowerment and emotional liberation.

Through forgiveness, I create a space for healing and transformation. The darkness of adultery does not have to shadow our family permanently. My worth transcends the actions of others; it's rooted in my strength and capacity to heal.

As I write this reflection, I affirm that I am more than the pain caused by the family secrets that involved adultery with a family friend. I am a vessel of resilience, growth, and unwavering determination. Through forgiveness, I break free from the chains of the past and stride confidently into a future shaped by my choices.

With compassion and strength,

[Your Name]

Meditative Thought of the Day

Vulnerability isn't weakness; it's an armor of authenticity. I reveal my true self through vulnerability, fostering connections rooted in truth and empathy.

Deeper Connection Within

1. What would you say to your younger self who experienced the pain caused by these family secrets?

_____
_____
_____
_____
_____
_____

2. How do you see your personal growth contributing to healing your family dynamic?

_____
_____
_____
_____
_____
_____

3. How can you actively cultivate gratitude for the lessons learned and the strength you've gained from this journey?

_____
_____
_____
_____
_____
_____

Loving Statements About Me

I am forgiving myself for any self-blame I carried due to family secrets.

I am rewriting my story with the pen of courage and the ink of resilience.

I am worthy of forgiveness and acceptance, both from myself and others.

Gratitude Reflection of the Day

Today, I honor the wisdom that has blossomed, guiding me toward choices that promote healing and well-being.

Inner Reflections

Forgiveness For Illegitimate Children

Forgiveness Reflection of the Day

Dear Me,

In the realm of family secrets surrounding illegitimate children, I embark on a journey of healing and forgiveness. Through this transformative act, I extend compassion to those who held these secrets and myself as I navigate the complexities of emotions that have arisen.

I forgive myself for moments of confusion and self-blame that clouded my understanding. Just as I extend empathy to others, I direct that same empathy inward. I release the burden of self-condemnation and replace it with the understanding that I, too, deserve healing and grace.

As I traverse this healing path, I recognize that the shroud of secrecy around illegitimate children does not define my worth or the essence of our family. While these hidden truths have cast shadows, they need not dictate the entirety of our story. Through forgiveness, I release the emotional weight they have placed upon me.

I forgive those who chose to keep the secret of illegitimate children, acknowledging the intricate web of emotions and circumstances that influenced their decisions. As I strive to understand within myself, I extend that understanding to them.

Forgiveness is confronting my emotions, facing them head-on, and ultimately releasing their grip on my heart. Each step towards forgiveness signifies a step towards personal empowerment and emotional liberation.

Through forgiveness, I pave the way for healing and transformation. The veil of secrecy surrounding illegitimate children does not have to cast a permanent shadow over our family. My worth transcends the actions of others; it's rooted in my strength and capacity to heal.

As I write this reflection, I affirm that I am more than the pain caused by the family secrets surrounding illegitimate children. I am a vessel of resilience, growth, and unwavering determination. Through forgiveness, I break free from the chains of the past and stride confidently into a future shaped by my choices.

With compassion and strength,

[Your Name]

Meditative Thought of the Day

While I can't control the actions of others, I am responsible for my choices. My decisions shape my journey, which I navigate with purpose, integrity, and self-awareness.

Deeper Connection Within

1. How might your capacity for forgiveness inspire others in their healing journeys?

_____
_____
_____
_____
_____
_____

2. What elements of nature or spirituality can you connect with to find solace and strength?

_____
_____
_____
_____
_____
_____

3. How can you shift your perspective from victimhood to empowerment as you navigate this journey?

_____
_____
_____
_____
_____
_____

Loving Statements About Me

I am building a life reflecting my true self and boundless potential.

I am stepping into my power and embracing the journey of healing.

I am rewriting my family's narrative with strength and self-love.

Gratitude Reflection of the Day

I appreciate the sense of liberation that comes from forgiving and releasing the weight of generational wounds.

Inner Reflections

Forgiveness For Financial Deception

Forgiveness Reflection of the Day

Dear Me,

As I embark on a journey of healing and forgiveness from the web of family secrets surrounding financial deception, I extend compassion to those who chose to deceive and to myself as I navigate the intricate maze of emotions that have surfaced.

I forgive myself for moments of confusion and self-blame that shrouded my understanding. Just as I extend empathy to others, I direct that same empathy inward. I release the grip of self-condemnation and replace it with the understanding that I, too, deserve healing and grace.

In the healing process, I acknowledge that the cloak of secrecy around financial deception does not define my worth or the essence of our family. While these hidden truths have cast shadows, they need not dictate the entirety of our story. Through forgiveness, I release the emotional burden they have placed upon me.

I forgive those who engaged in financial deception, recognizing the complex emotions and circumstances that influenced their decisions. As I strive to understand within myself, I extend that understanding to them.

Forgiveness is confronting my emotions, facing them head-on, and ultimately deciding to release their hold on my heart. Each step towards forgiveness signifies a step towards personal empowerment and emotional liberation.

Through forgiveness, I create a space for healing and transformation. The darkness of financial deception does not have to shroud our family permanently. My worth transcends the actions of others; it's rooted in my strength and capacity to heal.

As I put pen to paper, I affirm that I am more than the pain caused by the family secrets surrounding financial deception. I am a vessel of resilience, growth, and unwavering determination. Through forgiveness, I free myself from the chains of the past and stride confidently into a future shaped by my choices.

With compassion and strength,

[Your Name]

Meditative Thought of the Day

Forgiveness is the song of my heart, sung in harmony with my healing. I extend it to others but also to myself. Through forgiveness, my heart becomes a resilient sanctuary of growth.

Deeper Connection Within

1. What practices or activities bring you joy and can help you cultivate positive emotions?

_____

_____

_____

_____

_____

_____

2. How can you communicate your boundaries and needs to family members as you navigate this journey?

_____

_____

_____

_____

_____

_____

3. What fears or apprehensions arise when you consider fully embracing the process of forgiveness?

_____

_____

_____

_____

_____

_____

Loving Statements About Me

I am releasing the grip of the past and moving forward with confidence.

I am empowered to create a new story that honors my worth and growth.

I am rewriting my story with authenticity, vulnerability, and self-compassion.

Gratitude Reflection of the Day

I'm thankful for the opportunity to break the chains of the past and create a legacy of love, healing, and resilience.

Inner Reflections

DAY 20

Forgiveness For Deception About Maternal Or Paternal Parents

Forgiveness Reflection of the Day

Dear Me,

In the realm of family secrets that revolve around deception about paternal or maternal parents, I embark on a journey of healing and forgiveness. Through this transformative act, I extend compassion to those who concealed the truth and myself as I navigate the intricate web of emerging emotions.

I forgive myself for moments of confusion and self-blame that clouded my understanding. Just as I extend empathy to others, I direct that same empathy inward. I release the burden of self-condemnation and replace it with the understanding that I, too, deserve healing and grace.

As I tread this healing path, I recognize that the shroud of secrecy around parental identity does not define my worth or the essence of our family. While these hidden truths have cast shadows, they need not dictate the entirety of our story. Through forgiveness, I release the emotional weight they have placed upon me.

I forgive those who chose to keep the secret of parental identity, acknowledging the intricate emotions and circumstances that influenced their decisions. As I strive to understand within myself, I extend that understanding to them.

Forgiveness is confronting my emotions, facing them head-on, and ultimately releasing their grip on my heart. Each step towards forgiveness signifies a step towards personal empowerment and emotional liberation.

Through forgiveness, I lay the groundwork for healing and transformation. The veil of secrecy surrounding parental identity does not have to cast a permanent shadow over our family. My worth transcends the actions of others; it's rooted in my strength and capacity to heal.

As I pen this reflection, I affirm that I am more than the pain caused by the family secrets about parental identity. I am a vessel of resilience, growth, and unwavering determination. Through forgiveness, I break free from the chains of the past and stride confidently into a future shaped by my choices.

With compassion and strength,

[Your Name]

Meditative Thought of the Day

Healing is not circumstantial; it's a deliberate choice. I choose to heal even if the circumstances are challenging. I am the architect of my restoration, crafting a life filled with authenticity and growth.

Deeper Connection Within

1. What aspects of your life would you like to reclaim and rebuild as you heal?

_____

_____

_____

_____

_____

_____

2. How might forgiveness contribute to your sense of personal empowerment and autonomy?

_____

_____

_____

_____

_____

3. What strategies can you employ to manage triggers and emotional responses related to these secrets?

_____

_____

_____

_____

_____

_____

Loving Statements About Me

I am worthy of happiness, love, and all life's blessings.

I am embracing my inner strength and using it to overcome any challenge.

I am letting go of the pain of the past and making space for my bright future.

Gratitude Reflection of the Day

I express gratitude for the inner strength and determination that have carried me through the healing challenges.

Inner Reflections

Forgiveness For Criminal Past

Forgiveness Reflection of the Day

Dear Me,

As I embark on a path of forgiveness and healing from the weight of family secrets concerning a criminal past kept hidden, I extend compassion to myself and those who chose to shield this truth. Through this journey, I decide to release the burden of pain and find the strength to heal.

I forgive myself for moments of confusion and self-blame that shrouded my understanding. Just as I extend empathy to others, I direct that same empathy inward. I release the grip of self-condemnation and replace it with the understanding that I, too, deserve healing and grace.

Amidst this healing, I recognize that the veil of secrecy surrounding a criminal past does not define my worth or the core of our family. While these hidden truths may cast shadows, they need not dictate the entirety of our story. Through forgiveness, I relinquish the emotional weight they have placed upon me.

I forgive those who elected to hide their criminal past, acknowledging the intricate emotions and circumstances that influenced their decisions. As I strive to understand within myself, I extend that understanding to them.

Forgiveness is confronting my emotions, facing them head-on, and ultimately deciding to release their hold on my heart. Each step towards forgiveness signifies a step towards personal empowerment and emotional liberation.

Through forgiveness, I create space for healing and transformation. The darkness of a concealed criminal past does not have to shroud our family forever. My worth transcends the actions of others; it's rooted in my strength and capacity to heal.

As I write this reflection, I affirm that I am more than the pain caused by the family secrets concerning a criminal past. I am a vessel of resilience, growth, and unwavering determination. Through forgiveness, I unchain myself from the past and stride confidently into a future molded by my choices.

With compassion and strength,

[Your Name]

Meditative Thought of the Day

As I close this chapter, I open myself to the unwritten pages of empowerment. The secrets and revelations I've encountered are not my final destination. With every step, I am walking towards a future illuminated by healing, self-love, and the brilliant light of my resilience.

Deeper Connection Within

1. How can you find forgiveness within yourself without needing validation or understanding from others?

_____

_____

_____

_____

_____

2. How might your experiences with these secrets shape your capacity for empathy and compassion?

_____

_____

_____

_____

_____

3. How can you remind yourself that healing is a process and that every step forward is a triumph?

_____

_____

_____

_____

_____

Loving Statements About Me

I am reclaiming my voice and stepping into my authenticity with pride.

I am rewriting the script of my life with courage, grace, and empowerment.

I deserve all life's goodness and am ready to embrace it fully.

Gratitude Reflection of the Day

At this moment, I am filled with immense gratitude for the healing of generational wounds, for it has opened the door to a life of freedom, love, and boundless possibilities.

Inner Reflections

Transformation And Renewal

As you turn the final pages of this journal, you're not merely closing a chapter – you're concluding a profound journey of healing, self-discovery, and empowerment. Your commitment to confronting the dark and deep family secrets that have cast shadows over your life is an act of immense courage. It's a testament to your resilience, determination to heal, and unwavering belief in transformation's power.

Reclaiming Your Power

Discovering and confronting family secrets can be a seismic shift in your life, shattering the illusions and revealing the raw truths that were once hidden. Yet, within this upheaval lies the opportunity to reclaim your power. By facing the secrets head-on, you've taken a significant step toward breaking the chains that have bound you to the past. You've declared that you refuse to be defined solely by the kept secrets – you are a multifaceted individual who can rewrite your narrative.

Forging the Path of Healing

As you've journeyed through the pages of this journal, you've delved into the complexities of forgiveness, accountability, self-compassion, and rebuilding trust. You've unearthed layers of emotions, faced discomfort, and embraced vulnerability. Your willingness to traverse this healing path is a testament to your commitment to your well-being and growth. Remember, healing is not linear; it's a process that unfolds over time, with each step bringing you closer to the light.

Rebuilding Trust and Confidence

The healing process from family secrets involves more than just addressing the wounds caused by the revelations. It also entails rebuilding trust – both within yourself and in your relationships. Recognize that trust is earned through consistency, open communication, and genuine actions. You're actively participating in rebuilding trust by staying accountable for your role in the family dynamics, whether as a secret-keeper or as someone who uncovered the truth. This journey requires patience, understanding, and a commitment to growth.

Restoring Relationships

Discovering family secrets can lead to strained relationships, fractured bonds, and estrangement. However, as you've explored within these pages, restoring and nurturing these connections is possible. Honest conversations, active listening, and a willingness to acknowledge past hurts can create a renewed sense of connection. Remember that healing may require time, and rebuilding relationships is gradual. Approach it with empathy and a genuine desire for understanding.

Embracing Your Unique Journey

It's important to acknowledge that everyone's journey is unique. The insights and revelations you've gained from this journal are tailored to your experiences, emotions, and path. Embrace your journey with self-compassion and an open heart. Be patient with yourself as you navigate the complexities of forgiveness, healing, and growth. Trust that you possess the strength to overcome challenges and continue moving forward.

Walking Towards the Light

As you close this journal, remember that you're not walking away from the darkness but towards the light—the light of self-awareness, self-acceptance, and the potential for a brighter future. The healing journey is ongoing, and the tools and insights you've gained from these pages will guide you. Your transformation is a testament to your resilience and commitment to creating a life filled with authenticity, understanding, and growth.

Your Story Continues

As you step away from these words and embark on the next phase of your journey, remember that your story continues to unfold. The revelations, the pain, and the healing you've experienced are all integral parts of your narrative. Embrace your account with all its complexities, for it is uniquely yours. Your journey is a testament to your strength, growth capacity, and unwavering determination to heal and thrive.

With gratitude for sharing this journey,

Tuniscia O

Below Is A List Of All 35 Forgiveness Journals

Written By: Tuniscia Okeke

**Available on Amazon and other major bookstores or www.forgivenesslifestyle.com
Instagram: @forgiveness_lifestyle
For bulk orders: info@forgivenesslifestyle.com**

Forgiving Yourself

Forgiving Your Body Journal

Accepting the Gift of Forgiveness Journal

Forgiving People Who Reject You Journal

P.S. Forgive Yourself First Journal

Who Do You Struggle To Forgive Journal

Forgiving Your Struggle With Addiction Journal

Forgiving Your Parents

Forgiving Your Mother Journal

Forgiving Your Father Journal

Forgiving Your Parents Journal

Parenthood

Forgiving and Overcoming Mom Guilt Journal

Forgiveness Journal for Fathers

Parents Forgiving Tweens/Teen Journal

Parents Forgiving Adult Children Journal

Family

Forgiving Dead Loved One's Journal

Forgiving Family Secrets Journal

Forgiving The Bullies In Your Family Journal

Forgiving Your Siblings Journal

Marriage

Forgiving Your Wife Journal
Forgiving Your Husband Journal
Forgiving Your Mother-
In-Law Journal

Romantic Relationships

Forgiving Your Ex Journal
Forgiving The "New"
Woman Journal

Teens & Millennials

Forgiveness Journals for Teens
Forgiveness Journal
for Millennials

Religion

Forgiving God Journal
Forgiving Church People Journal

Blended Family

Forgiving A Co-Parent Journal
Forgiveness Journal
for Stepmothers
Forgiving Your
Stepmother Journal
Forgiving Your Stepkids
Mom Journal

Relationships

Forgiving Your Abuser Journal
Forgiving Friends Journal

Business/Finances

Forgiveness In Business Journal
Forgiving People At
Work Journal
Forgiving Past Money
Mistakes Journal

Sending you loving energy as you
forgive, heal, and grow.
www.forgivenesslifestyle.com

Thank You

Gratitude is the thread that weaves connections, and at this moment, I extend my most profound appreciation to those whose unwavering support and love have been the foundation of this 35-journal writing journey and beyond.

To my beloved husband, your unwavering confidence and support during our marriage and this writing project have been my anchor. Thank you for your belief in me. It has been a constant source of inspiration. Your love and presence in my life make my soul smile.

Your honesty and vulnerability to my mother led to this beautiful healing journey. Your transparency has supported my healing and given me the strength to support others on their transformational journey. I will forever be grateful for your courage to tell the truth.

My dear daughter, Shantia Dajah, your reminder to give myself grace has been a guiding light. Your wisdom transcends your years. You make my heart smile.

To my incredible son, Damien, your encouragement and motivation have fueled my determination to embark on this transformative journey. Your presence in my life is a source of boundless joy.

To Ike, my dynamic youngest son, your cheering from the sidelines has been a source of motivation and warmth. Your enthusiasm lights up my days.

My sister, Tanniedra, your unwavering belief in me and our brainstorming sessions have been invaluable. You are truly a gift.

Little sister, Jazmin, your willingness to share your experiences and vulnerability has touched my heart deeply. Your courage is inspiring.

To my "business bestie," Martha Banks Hall, the Creator of Vision Words, your prayers, encouraging texts, and our deep explorations of thoughts have been a source of clarity and growth to help me birth this project.

Denise, my beautiful friend, "The Fertility Godmother," your enthusiastic voice memos have made me feel like a rock star. Your presence has been a pillar of my strength.

To Thuy, I'm deeply grateful for your accountability and sisterhood, and I hold you as the beautiful gift you are close to my heart.

To Georgette and Cristal, your cheers have lifted my spirits. Your presence in my life is a blessing.

You all hold a special place in my heart, and I thank you from the depths of my soul for being a part of my journey.

Made in the USA
Middletown, DE
15 October 2023

40779107R00110